Wisdom & Wack FOR THE GRADUATE

For Maureen, my wife and best friend—these illustrations are for you.

– N.S.

For my parents, who first seeded my curiosity (and funded its growth).

– K.B.

978-1-933176-15-4

Published by Red Rock Press\
            New York, New York

            www.RedRockPress.com

Book design by Susan Smilanic SJS Designs

Library of Congress Cataloging-in-Publication Data

Wisdom and wack for the graduate / compiled by Kate Barth ;
illustrations
by Neil Shapiro.
     p. cm.
  ISBN-13: 978-1-933176-15-4
  1. College graduates–Conduct of life–Quotations, maxims, etc. 2.
Young adults–Conduct of life–Quotations, maxims, etc. 3. Graduation
(School)–Quotations, maxims, etc. 4. Baccalaureate
addresses–Miscellanea. I. Barth, Kate, 1982- II. Shapiro, Neil.
  BJ1661.W57 2006
  170'.44–dc22
                                        2006029384

Printed in Mexico

Wisdom & Wack FOR THE GRADUATE

Illustrations by **Neil Shapiro**
Edited by **Kate Barth**

RED ROCK PRESS

If you were graduating from Oxford University in England about 350 years ago you might have been dismayed to find out that your diploma depended on your deliverance of a well-rated commencement speech (in Latin—what else?). You could have been further put out to realize you had a very long afternoon in front of you as all of your classmates also had to give their speeches, and alas, the folding chair would not be invented for another several hundred years. However, a cheery thought might dart through your head: Should you prove yourself a second Cicero, chances were pretty high that you would be offered a nice ministerial job at a country parish far from the Black Plague-ravaged streets of London.

Today's commencement speeches aim to be somewhat less onerous on eager graduates, although as a recent speaker, Indra Nooyi, put it: "Some graduates–perhaps those who minored in self-awareness–refer to the commencement address as "the snooze before the booze."

Thinking back to my college graduation day, I must confess that between my nervousness as to whether my family would embarrass me with B. K. (i.e. Baby Kate) stories at the after-graduation luncheon and my fantasies of the fabulous job offers awaiting me just on the other side of commencement, I remember very little of what the Noble Peace prize-winning speaker said (although I'm fairly sure she encouraged us all to work towards a better, more peaceful world).

The real purpose of the commencement speech is to give the graduates-to-be one final piece of advice or a mission before the school relinquishes them forever—or at least until its next annual appeal. Such themes as "*Carpe Diem* [Seize the Day]," "the world is your oyster" or "the oyster is currently stuck in the mud—it's your task to dig it out" have proved distressingly common. Yet many illustrious commencement speakers realize that no matter how many prizes they've won, countries they've governed or gold records they've cut, the almost-graduates are often more interested in throwing off their caps than absorbing more nuggets of knowledge. The best speakers manage to wrestle back the students' attention through jokes and witticisms.

This book is a collection of the wisest and wackiest things said to high-school, college, business and law-school graduates in recent years. From Presidents to poets, from CEO's to rock stars, each speaker quoted here has imparted a pearly bit of something smart. So consider this a cheat sheet of advice from the funny and famous or, at least, successful, on surviving post-graduation life.

– Kate Barth

" I note that you are dressed in black. Why the gloom? "

– Richard H. Brodhead
Dean of Yale College

Yale University
New Haven, Connecticut
May 23, 2004

"
You must go. There's no more room for you here.
In fact, your rooms have already been rented . . .
Get used to it. This is your life. Whatever it is, it's
yours. And get on with it.

"

**– Rev. Peter J. Gomes
Baptist theologian**

University of North Carolina
Chapel Hill, North Carolina
May 16, 2006

"

The real world is not a restoration. If you see people in the real world making bricks out of straw and water, those people are not colonial re-enactors—they are poor. Help them.

"

– Jon Stewart
Comedy Central newscaster

College of William and Mary
Williamsburg, Virginia
May 24, 2004

WATCH THIS SITE

"Laugh as much as you can. Never take yourself too seriously.

– George J. Tenet
C.I.A. Director

Texas A & M
College Station, Texas
May 14, 2004

Remember the words of Lily Tomlin: 'If you win the rat race, you're still a rat.'

– Anna Quindlen
Writer

Mount Holyoke College
South Hadley. Mass.
May 23, 1999

The analogy of the five fingers as the five major continents leaves the long, middle finger for North America, and, in particular, the United States. As the longest of the fingers, it really stands out . . . if used inappropriately—just like the U.S. itself—the middle finger can convey a negative message and get us in trouble. You know what I'm talking about.

**– Indra Nooyi
PepsiCo President**

Columbia University Business School
New York, New York
May 15, 2005

When people show you who they are, believe them, the first time. Not the 29th time! That is particularly good when it comes to men situations.

– Oprah Winfrey
Talk show host and
magazine publisher

Wellesley College
Wellesley, Mass.
May 30, 1997

This, then, is what I learned on my own graduation day . . . which I pass onto you: Those who would reject you because you are wearing the wrong shoes are not worth being accepted by . . . Kneel before no man.

– Salman Rushdie
Novelist, targeted for death in 1989
by the Ayatollah Khomeni.
Iran lifted the fatwah in 1998.

Bard College
Annandale-on-Hudson, N. Y.
May 25, 1996

"

A commencement speech is a particularly difficult assignment. The speaker is given no topic and is expected to be able to inspire all the graduates with a stirring speech about nothing at all. I suppose that's why so many lawyers are asked to be commencement speakers; they're in the habit of talking extensively even when they have nothing to say.

"

**– Sandra Day O'Connor
U.S. Supreme Court Judge**

Stanford University
Palo Alto, California
June 13, 2004

"

As we say in the wetlands, 'Ribbit-ribbit-kneedeep-ribbit,' which means: May success and a smile always be yours . . . even when you're knee deep in the sticky muck of life.

"

**– Kermit the Frog
Muppet**

Southampton College
Southampton, New York
May 19, 1996

It is harder to put your foot in your mouth when your have your pen in your hand.

– **William Safire**
Richard Nixon speechwriter,
New York Times columnist

Syracuse University
Syracuse, N. Y.
May 13, 1978

Avoid jellyfish.

Wayne Coyne
Rock musician

Classen [High] School
Oklahoma City, Oklahoma
May 25, 2006

Let me begin with a very valuable lesson I've learned – a lesson that has influenced my well-being – and here it is: Listen to your mother.

– George W. Bush
President of the United States

Louisiana State University
Baton Rouge, Louisiana
May 21, 2004

In all circumstances, wear comfortable shoes. You never know when you may have to run for your life.

– Callie Khouri
Screenplay writer

Sweet Briar College
Sweet Briar, Virginia
May 22, 1994

You are the most coddled generation in history. I belong to the last generation that did not have to be in a car seat . . . But you seem nice enough, so I'll try to give you some advice. First of all, when you go to apply for your first job, don't wear these robes. Medieval garb does not instill confidence in future employers – unless you're applying to be a scrivener. And if someone does offer you a job, say yes. You can always quit later.

– Stephen Colbert
Comedian, satiric newscaster

Knox College
Galesburg, Illinois
June 3, 2006

There's no guarantee you will ever again spend each day surrounded by so many highly intelligent people.

– **Samuel L. Jackson**
Actor

Vassar College
Poughkeepsie, New York
May 23, 2004

And above all, party on, Demon Deacons, party on.

– Colin L. Powell
U.S. Secretary of State

Wake Forest University
Wake Forest, North Carolina
May 17, 2004

"

Now you are free. Free of the pressure of exams. Free to begin the next stage of your life. And free to pay back your student loans.

"

**– Kofi Annan
U. N. Secretary General**

Massachusetts Institute of Technology (M.I.T.)
Cambridge, Mass.
June 6, 1997

Rule One: Get yourself in the game. Ever watch a little kid standing courtside while the big kids play basketball? When a ball goes out of bounds, he or she runs for it and passes it back in. As time goes on, when an older kid has to get home for dinner, somebody yells 'Hey! Wanna play?' That's it, the heart of it really.

– Christopher Matthews
TV Host – Hardball

Hobart and William Smith Colleges
Geneva, New York
May 16, 2004

Sending kids off to college is a lot like putting them in the witness protection program. If the person who comes out is easily recognizable as the same person who went in, something has gone terribly, dangerously wrong.

– Richard Russo
Novelist

Colby College
Waterville, Maine
May 23, 2004

> The next step: you need to find a career and create a life for yourself. That's why I highly encourage all of you to play in the NBA—it's a great life.

– Steve Kerr
Basketball star

University of Arizona
Tucson, Arizona
May 15, 2004

"It was Conrad Hilton, the hotel millionaire, who was asked toward the end of his long and successful career for some lessons he had learned, something that might be a guide to the young. After a long pause, he said he thought one really good idea was to keep the shower curtain inside the tub.

**– Roger Mudd
T.V. newscaster**

Randolph Macon College
Ashland, Virginia
May 19, 2004

Sometimes the road stretches straight ahead. Sometimes you're stuck in 5 o'clock traffic. Sometimes you're just trying to find the nearest exit.

– **Margaret Spellings**
U.S. Secretary of Education

Montgomery College
Montgomery, Maryland
May 17, 2006

Have some children. Children add texture to your life. They will save you from turning into old fogies before you're middle-aged. They will teach you humility . . . When you reach the golden years, your best bet is children, the ingrates.

– Russell Baker
Humorist and essayist

Connecticut College
New London, Connecticut
May 27, 1995

The sight of a rock star in academic robes is a bit like when people put their King Charles spaniels in little tartan sweats and hats. It's not natural, and it doesn't make the dog any smarter.

– Bono
Rock Star

University of Pennsylvania
Philadelphia, Pennsylvania
May 17, 2003

"

Everyone has a weird roommate. If you don't have a weird roommate, then you're the weird room mate.

"

– Conan O'Brien
T.V. Talk Show Host

Stuyvesant High School
New York, New York
June 26, 2006

Become a TV producer – why not? – it works for me . . . Oh ... you mean everyone doesn't want to be a TV producer? Well, okay then, go into medicine. Don't like blood? Okay, how about computers? . . . The Internet . . . Want a job in the travel industry? Join NASA . . . Be a train engineer . . . Become a pilot.

– Marcy A Mcginnis
CBS Senior Vice President

Marymount University
Arlington Virginia
May 8, 2005

I want to express my deep appreciation and my congratulations to all those students who are receiving degrees and certificates. I think this is the first time in the States I am receiving an honorary degree in an actual ceremony of convocation when the students are also receiving their degrees. So I am particularly happy today. Of course, another factor in my particular joy is that you had to work hard to get it for many years, whereas I didn't have to study at all!

– The Dalai Lama
Tibetan Buddhist Leader

Emory University
Atlanta, Georgia
May 1998

So, what's it like in the real world? Well, the food is better, but beyond that, I don't recommend it.

– Bill Watterson
Creator of *Calvin and Hobbes*

Kenyon College
Gambier, Ohio
May 20, 1990

The muse is a sweet idea, like the tooth fairy. The muse supposedly comes down like lightning and fills your fingers with the necessary voltage to type up something brilliant. But nobody ever made a living depending on a muse.

– Ann Patchett
Novelist

Sarah Lawrence College
Bronxville, New York
May 19, 2006

In future years, you will recall this ceremony and you will understand that today was the day you first began to forget everything you learned in college.

– Judith A McHale
CEO of Discovery Communications

American University Kogod School of Business
Washington D.C.
May 8th, 2005

Let me put it this way. I can find out where you live. I have my resources. And if I show up at your house ten years from now and find nothing in your living room but *The Readers Digest*, nothing on your bedroom night table but the newest Dan Brown novel, and nothing in your bathroom but *Jokes for the John*, I'll chase you down to the end of your driveway and back, screaming, 'Where are your books? You graduated college ten years ago, so how come there are no damn books in your house? Why are you living on the intellectual equivalent of Kraft Macaroni and Cheese?'

– Stephen King
Novelist

University of Maine
Orono, Maine
May 7, 2005

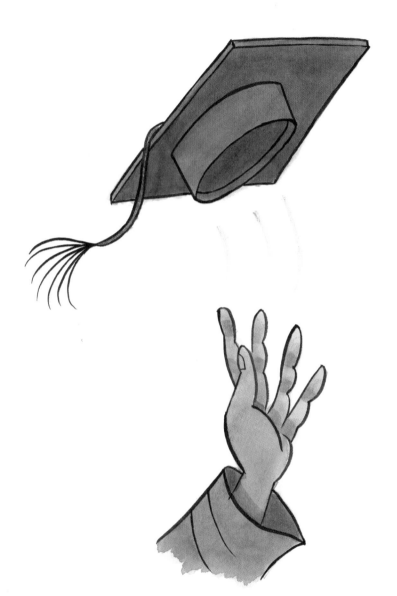